MY FLIRTATION
WITH INTERNATIONAL SOCIALISM

First published in 2010 by
The Dedalus Press
13 Moyclare Road
Baldoyle
Dublin 13
Ireland

www.dedaluspress.com

Editor: Pat Boran

ISBN 978 1 906614 29 4

Dedalus Press titles are represented in North America by
Syracuse University Press, Inc., 621 Skytop Road,
Suite 110, Syracuse, New York 13244,
and in the UK by
Central Books, 99 Wallis Road, London E9 5LN

Cover image © afhunta / iStockphoto.com

The Dedalus Press receives financial assistance from
The Arts Council / An Chomhairle Ealaíon

MY FLIRTATION
WITH INTERNATIONAL SOCIALISM

Gerry Murphy

DEDALUS PRESS
DUBLIN, IRELAND

ACKNOWLEDGEMENTS

Acknowledgements are due to the editors of the following in which a number of these poems, or versions of them, previously appeared:

Poetry Ireland Review, Southword, The SHOp, The Stinging Fly, and *The Cork Review.*

Thanks are due to Billy Ramsell for a close reading of the manuscript.

for Fiona Barry

Contents

NOTHING IS LOST / 9

NOTHING IS LOST

after Randall Jarrell

As if my mother
stepped from the shuffling throng
on South Main Street
and stood before me:
"Dead? Who told you I was dead?"

New Arrivals Eighth Circle

But who are you, whose cheeks
are sorely runneled by such copious tears?
What hideous garment shines on your stooped shoulders?

And he replied: "This glowing Charvet shirt
is lead-lined and sizzles against my skin.
And so heavy it creaks likes a disused conscience."

The King

after Cavafy — for Jack Healy

When the Macedonians deserted him,
preferring Pyrrhos,
Dimitrios, so they said,
didn't behave at all like a king.
He took off his golden robes,
pulled on a peasant's cloak
and slipped out of the city.
Just like an actor really,
as if all those years as king
meant little or nothing,
apart from an interesting role.

April Morning, English Market

for Kay Harte

Mid-morning lull
in the market,
a butcher
rocks back and forth
on his heels
awaiting the noonday rush.
A breeze plays across
the empty scales,
the digital display,
alert to its vagaries,
registers their weight
as they flit past.

Farewell to a Pagan

i.m. Gregory O'Donoghue

The fox presented itself at the roundabout,
its splendid golden pelt
smeared across two lanes.
Only yesterday we saw you off
without the prescribed rituals,
the church so packed
with the great and the good,
we couldn't very well set it alight,
toss that crabby priest
back into the flames
and let the ensuing conflagration
be your all-consuming pyre.
Only yesterday we let you down,
colluding in the standard Catholic guff
without a yelp of protest.
And so I summon this fabled beast
to accompany you into the afterlife.
He will guide you like wily Odysseus
through dense thickets of murmuring shades
begging for news of the world.
He will leave you with the poets,
still defending the proper rigour of the canon,
still jostling fiercely in the pecking order,
still falling out …

Capaneus

Who is that, stretched out yonder, all rippling muscle,
steeling himself against the constant flame,
as if the fiery hail would merely glance off him?

Lowering his voice, Virgil turned to me and said:
"That is Capaneus, one of the seven kings who invested
Thebes, he held and obviously still holds

God in some contempt and flaunts it ceaselessly,
but, as I told him, his frothing blasphemies make
a fitting badge for such an obdurate breast."

The Monks

after Hewitt's 'From The Tibetan' — for William Wall

In my native province when I was young,
the monks were presumed to be crooked.
Not that they were intrinsically less honest than the rest of us,
just that their calling gave them unlimited opportunities for *graft*.

They were not expected to be intellectuals or indeed poets,
after all, they were not exactly bright or even educated,
ideas were as scarce as books in their satchels.
Don't get me wrong, they knew the rituals by heart
and when called for, intoned the proper chants
at weddings and funerals, turned the prayer wheels vigorously
and could belt out *The Emperor's Tunic* or *The Great Wall of China*
with the best of them.

For the rest of their time it was understood
that they would work at rewarding their families:
finding jobs for their nephews, accepting donations from
contractors
and generally building up their assets.
This was all done with a great show of cordiality,
featuring handclasps, salutes, finger-signals and arcane passwords,
to give the impression of the necessity of complicated manoeuvres
for the success of ordinary transactions.

Now, in middle-age, I live in the capital.
I find the monks here are just as crooked, if not more so,
although the tedious work of feathering their nests
is done on their behalf by a permanent bureaucracy,
leaving them more time to devote to politics.
This compels them to acquire a more sophisticated vocabulary,
leading one or two of them to publish books.
This development would be considered extravagant
in my old home but not in the least surprising.

Lunch at The Farm Gate

i.m. Michael Davitt

You'd think—
given the day that was in it,
given the hour that was upon us—
we would have selected
cold meats, chilled drinks,
cool dripping salads.
But no,
everyone at the table
called for hot steaming plates
as you were licked into nothingness
by the voracious flames
of the crematorium furnace.

Purgatory

after Henry VIII

You would do as well
to seek for it
in the tale of Robin Hood,
as to find it in Scripture.

At Mount Melleray

after Seán Dunne

Carp ripples spread
across the monastery pond,
a one-note rook
scratches the silence.

Sweeney's Bower

after Gerard Murphy — for Cliona Kearney

My little oratory
in the ivied tree-top,
I wouldn't swap it for a mansion.
The stars obediently follow
the sun and the moon
above its leafy canopy,
and though its roof is the sky itself,
neither the wind nor the rain
trouble it.

After Reading Geoffrey Hill

Diluvial rain,
clouds the colour of pewter
loiter above the Cumner Hills.
A gap in the heavens—
to let through what exactly?—
a forced fart of blood and feathers,
the dove and her urgent reply
blended, free of charge,
in a passing jet turbine.

Who wants a clean slate anyway?

Reading with Delanty

after Wordsworth — for Patricia Ferreira

At night,
when the moon was silvering the slate-topped roofs,
we'd steal out, and for the best part of the hours of darkness,
stroll the quiet streets or the paths along the river,
repeating favourite verses with one voice,
or making up more as tricky as the bats
that flitted too close for comfort 'round our heads.
Well might we be glad, lifted above the earth
by such ephemeral fancies, brighter than plain madness
or the empty, swirling promises of wine.
And though often the objects of our passion
were false and somewhat overwrought,
neither did we stoop to mere vulgarity.
Nothing less than Truth herself was working in us,
guiding us to her nobler summits.
Why wonder then if sounds of exultation
echoed through the streets or across the water?
Everything we said or did
in that delirious world of poetry
was suspended in a festive, never-ending moment,
beyond the reach of time or quotidian stain.

Thursday July 31st 1800

after Dorothy Wordsworth

I was busy all morning making fair copies.
In the stifling heat of the afternoon Coleridge arrived,
carrying the second volume of *Lyrical Ballads.*
William and Coleridge went to bathe in the lake,
to the sounds of much splashing and shouting.
Afterwards, we sailed down to Loughrigg,
reading poems aloud on the water,
letting the boat take its own course.

In the Retirement Home

after David Cavanagh

Neil Armstrong
leans back in his rocker
and points at the moon.
"I've been there!" he declares.
"Of course you have," replies the nurse,
"of course you have…"

It Takes All Types

after Inuo Taguchi

Some men can survive
with a packet of cigarettes,
a magnifying glass
and nail clippers.

Others insist on a military rank,
war-clouds lowering over a designated city
and a secret bunker in the desert.

Me?
a whirlwind in the kitchen,
relentlessly dismantling the entire Universe.

Appeal

for Dave O'Keefe

"Which earthquake?"
I enquired of the shopkeeper,
pointing to the donations box.
"I'm not sure,"
he replied,
"probably the most recent,
or possibly the one before that,
some fucking earthquake anyway!"

In Mid-Stream

for Conal Creedon

I meet the novelist on Christy Ring Bridge.
We swap the usual literary gossip:
who's up, who's going down, who's definitely out.
I show him my recently published poem,
prominently displayed in a distinguished journal,
which he reads leaning over the parapet
as the hooting traffic crawls past.
Suddenly self-conscious, he remarks,
that if anyone realizes we are discussing literature
they will think we're complete freaks.
I wouldn't mind, he says,
if we were doing something normal
like a drug-deal.

Free Kick

That boy racer,
who sped through the red lights
at the pedestrian-crossing
and gave the *finger* to your futile protest,
has just slammed into a low-loader
fifty metres farther up the road.
His severed head
is rolling back down the slight incline
as we speak
and will soon wobble to a halt
within reach of your primed right boot.

Three Borgesean Fragments

for Tom McCarthy

1. IT IS WRITTEN

The history of the universe
(including that sorry paragraph
on human existence)
is a tattered user's manual,
written by a minor, disaffected god
for the amusement of demons.

2. THE MAN WHOSE LIBRARY CARD EXPIRED

I have been travelling
for nights without cease
down dimly-lit corridors
stretching into infinity,
lined from skirting-board
to ceiling with innumerable
books which catalogue
the world from beginning
to end without catching
sight of a single librarian.

3. Does God Breathe?

The mind of God
is teeming with particulars,
past and future fused together
in a terrifying present.
He does not deign to think,
to think is to ignore,
to abstract, to generalize.
Anathema to Him
Who dwells fully
in the first dizzy particle,
in the last inert detail.

Unbestimmtheit

after Fiona Healy

According to Heisenberg,
we can never determine the exact position of Memphis,
or confidently declare the definitive momentum of Mullinavat.
Hey! Mr. Schrödinger, did you put out the cat?

A Book of Hours

after Lorca — for Maeve McLoughlin

ONE MORNING

The sky pulled off its blindfold
and a thousand-eyed dragon
licked us with tongues of flame.
The stars flickered out
in the dull glances of the crowd
and I remembered a sweetheart
I had never met.

SUMMER AFTERNOON

The girl on the swing
heads north to south,
south to north,
a squeaking pendulum.
Locked in that perfect parabola,
she traces the long return journeys
of the constellations.

A Minute to Midnight

Everyone is staring
at the clock,
eager for the New Year.
But like a child
who has fallen
down a well,
the New Year is shivering and shaking
as if trying to ask:
"Can we do this tomorrow?"

Only a Matter of Time

after Yasuhiro Yotsumoto

"I'm off,"
chirps our five year old son
as he slams the front door
and sets out for school in the morning.

"It's only me,"
croaks our thirty-five year old son
as he dumps his school-bag
in the hallway in the afternoon.

No Time Like the Present...

Ifeverythinghappensatonceyou'vegotemailGilgamesh.

No Time Like the Present...

for Marcella Reardon

On the star-ship,
the captain's wife
is eating an apple,
plucked,
a moment ago,
in Eden.

A Random History of the Desmond Rebellion

after Richard Berleth — for Cristina Gambra

ENTER SPENSER

Limerick 1577.
Hardly has he set foot in Ireland
when Spenser is swept up in a crowd
rushing to see the last act in the execution
of a local renegade.
The man had been hanged and disembowelled
and the quartering was about to begin.
"The traitor was called Murrogh O'Brien
and I saw an old woman who was his foster mother
take up his head whilst he was quartered
and suck up all the blood running thereout,
saying that the earth was not worthy to drink it
and therewith also steeping her face and breasts
and torn hair, crying and shrieking most terribly."

November 24TH 1579

Desmond was not done with Youghal,
not by a long shot.
Anything of worth was looted,
the walls were demolished
and everything else reduced to ashes.
The men who survived
were given the choice of joining
the Earl's army or being hacked to death
by the gallowglass.
The women were divided into lots
and assigned to the clans and companies.
When Thomas Butler entered the town
a few weeks later he found the smouldering ruins
in the sole keeping of a friar.

Weary of chasing shadows through treacherous
Munster bogs, Sir John Perrot challenged James Fitzmaurice
to single combat, winner take all.
Fitzmaurice accepted the gauntlet on condition
that he name the terms of combat.
He insisted on Irish ponies, light armour,
Irish dress and broad-bladed swords.
Sir John agreed to the conditions
and on the appointed day took up position
in a clearing in Kilmore Wood outside Kilmallock.
He waited from early morning until noon
when it began to rain heavily,
whereupon he decided to leave as Fitzmaurice
had obviously no intention of meeting him.
As Perrot turned to go an Irish messenger
galloped up to him with a letter from Fitzmaurice:
"If I do kill the great Sir John Perrot,
the Queen of England will but send another
in his stead to this province, but if he kill me
there is none to succeed me and command as I do."
Fitzmaurice had played Perrot for a fool,
the image of the Lord President of Munster
in Irish battle dress on an Irish pony
would never be forgotten in Ireland
or forgiven in England.

They call this "hewing" and "paunching",
a sword slash to the neck or a pike thrust
to the belly, the usual method of mass despatch
in the late 16th Century.
This was reserved for the Italian prisoners,
the Irish were hanged, drawn and quartered
and expected no less as rebels to the Crown.
The officers of the day, Mackworth and Raleigh,
led two hundred troops into the defeated fort
and slaughtered the entire garrison.
Their bodies were heaved over the cliff
onto the beach for easy burial.
Lord Grey who refused quarter
to the surrendering troops and
ordered their execution was heard to remark:
"Here lay as gallant and as goodly personages
as ever I have seen."

HEAD COUNT

Lord Grey's last venture into the wilderness
was in pursuit of the O'Connors
who had gone on a rampage in County Offaly.
Their most celebrated victim was Humphrey Mackworth,
notorious for his part in the slaughter at Fort Del Oro.
The O'Connors, well aware of his infamy,
gave him a slow agonizing death.
He had been flayed alive and imaginatively mutilated.
Grey came across his flyblown remains,
a few scraps of flesh and bones
lashed to a tree and crawling with rats.
Grey struck out as best he could
at the families of the O'Connors,
left at his mercy in their retreat into the bogs.
He brought fifty heads back to Dublin.
Subsequently recalled to London,
he was quietly relieved of his command.

Taking physic at his cottage in the Spring of 1583,
a mere six miles from Dublin,
Lodowick Bryskett is joined by some friends.
These include John Long, Archbishop of Armagh;
Chief Justice Sir Robert Dillon; Sir Warham St. Leger;
Captains Thomas Norris and Christopher Carleill;
Edmund Spenser and a nameless Dublin apothecary.
From Bryskett's account of the meeting
in his 'Discourse of Civil Life' we learn that
Spenser is busy on 'The Faerie Queen',
that the country is quieter because Grey
has "plowed and harrowed the rough ground"
and that a new nation is soon to be raised
by men educated in moral and natural philosophy.
Beyond the window the Wicklow hills are visible,
still wild, unconquered and teeming with rebels,
blissfully unaware of this charming vision
of the Renaissance finally arriving in Ireland.

Uneasy Lies The Head

The Earl was finally captured
on the slopes of Caherconree Mountain,
his retinue reduced to a mad priest
and a mangy dog.
In the struggle to secure him
his arm was broken
and it was decided to decapitate him
on the spot rather than carry him
kicking and screaming to Castleisland.
His head fetched one thousand
pieces of silver for Maurice O'Moriarty,
a loyal Queen's man
whose family had earlier been robbed
and abused by the Earl's rampaging followers.
The head was sent
to the Earl of Ormond in Kilkenny
and thence to London.
Elizabeth is said to have spent
an entire morning in quiet contemplation
of the grisly trophy
before having it spiked on London Bridge.

Epigram for a Windy Night

after the Irish, 18th century — for Billy Ramsell

The world laid low and the wind blowing,
hither and thither, the dust of Alexander and Caesar.
Tara buried under pasture and as for Troy...
And even the English—they too, like us—will die.

A Difficult Guest

after Cicero

What a relief,
to speed so formidable a guest
on his way without a wisp of trouble
on the horizon.
Caesar proved altogether most affable.
Need I say more?
We behaved like human beings together.
However, he's not the sort of person
to whom you would say:
"Be sure to call again on your way back"—
once is quite enough.
We talked mainly about literature
and the weather, this weird weather of late.
What did you expect, politics?
In short, I would venture to say,
he was entirely at his ease throughout.

from **Venetian Epigrams**

after Goethe — for Massimo Scimmi

This is the Italy I left!
Clouds of dust on the roads,
brigands in the mountain passes
and the thoroughly swindled tourist
turning out his emptied pockets
for the sullen frontier guards.
One looks in vain for German rectitude.
There is life and movement here
but little order and no discipline.
Everybody out of themselves,
at the expense of everybody else.
And those who finally attain power
invariably pull the ladder up after them
when they climb into the cockpit of State.

The Way Forward

after Brecht

Following the recent election,
with its paltry turnout
and appalling results,
the Government declared
that the People has finally
forfeited its confidence.
So it dissolved them
and formed another.

Memories of 'El Jefe' and the Cuban Revolution

for Seán Ó Murchu

Our guide is giving us
a potted history of the Revolution
as we make our way
from Havana to Playa Giron,
clipping happily
along the empty highway
in a small blue bus.
Each monument we pass
evokes a stirring anecdote,
featuring heavily outnumbered Fidelistas
defeating the reactionary hirelings of Batista.
At length, his heroic litany exhausted,
he calls for questions.
Sean, our leader, pipes up:
"Where can we get Mass...?

Red Cavalry in the Rain

after a painting by Bunin — for Manuel Villar Raso

The three outriders
have crossed the puddled, marshy ground
beyond the edge of the forest
and made it to the road without incident.
They ride with their sodden greatcoats
buttoned at the neck,
their left sleeves rising up
over their shoulders
sheathing their rifles.
Behind them at some distance
and still blurred in mist,
the vanguard
looms from the shadows
of the steadily dripping trees.

Militia Women

after Mao

How fearless they look,
shouldering shiny Kalashnikovs,
marching in formation
across a parade ground
lit by the first glints of morning.
China's daughters love their uniforms,
especially when they're designed in Paris.

Night and the Muse

after Juan De La Cruz

On a moonless night in a flare of longing
I slipped out unnoticed
by my sleeping neighbours.

Disguised by utter darkness,
I descended to the silent garden
and walked out into the fields.

Guided by an inner light
that blazed without illumination,
I passed in shadow.

And there, alone by the river,
your hair ruffled by stray night breezes,
I found you.

Laying your head on my shoulder,
your gentle touch overwhelmed me
and I lost track of my senses.

I came to, leaning against you,
my cares cast aside,
forgotten amongst the brambles.

Morning in Cefalù

I know
we fell asleep
spooning
but sometime
in the night
you turned
and now I wake
to find you
facing into me,
your forehead
level with my chin,
your breath
damp on my throat.
Lovely as you are,
lulled beyond reach
of the first stirrings
in the morning air,
I cannot help but
kiss you awake.

Septet at the End of Time

for Angelique

IMPERIAL FALL

I left the party,
deaf to the traffic in the street,
lost in the steady blue light
of your stare,
stumbling over my own rapt feet
all the way home.
My head already turned,
my heart inched open.

DARKROOM

So I develop this "thing" for you.
You, who already feature in that
amber-lit gallery of erotica: half-sleep.
Not that you know anything of this,
nor that you have since invaded
the long-disused darkroom of desire,
burning the red light into the small hours,
your face forming and re-forming
in the suddenly flaring trays.

Bemused

I am about to enter
my pin number on the key-pad
when your name flashes up
on the screen.
The shop assistant, noticing my hesitation,
asks if everything is all right.
"It's nothing," I reply
"probably a hallucination,
I got a bang on the head recently."
I enter my pin number
and purchase the book:
Fifty-seven ways to recognise the Muse...

BREDIN STREET

A battalion of discarded hair-clips
lies in disarray in the bathroom sink,
telling me your beautiful hair is loose,
tumbling over your shoulders,
spilling between your breasts,
catching a gleam of streetlight
through the bedroom window
as you turn down the duvet,
under which I will soon join you,
kissing your accumulated cares
into an all too temporary cease-fire,
holding you tight against Time
and its casual depredations,
growing younger and younger
in your arms.

Even the Elements

Even that summer wind—
whipping up off the river,
twisting through the hazel trees,
snapping your dress
taut around your body
in a sudden embrace—
wants you.

When it comes to missing you,
and it will—
after all it's been almost a week,
not counting two days travelling—
I could write with a shovel
dipped in axle-grease
on a pebble-dashed, gable-wall
and it would come out
as Chinese calligraphy on pure silk.
It only takes a word:
Drogheda naturally or train or eye-shadow
or tee-shirt or ear-ring or smooth
or kisses—oh God those kisses!—
even Cromwell will do it.
Anything to do with anything to do
with you.

FINGERS OF RAIN

If I cannot be with you,
then at least let me be
that occasional glint
in your full-cerulean eyes;
a whispered caress that moistens
your partly opened mouth;
the itch that makes you scratch
your beloved nose;
fingers of rain
in your wind-tousled hair;
escalating pressure of hands
on your breasts, your belly, your buttocks,
the briny hollows at the backs of your knees,
the slightly raised arches of your feet;
or, those tattooed lips on your upper, inner thigh,
yawning awake, then kissing and kissing and kissing
and kissing and kissing and kissing and kissing.

Matins

Stop me if I get this right:
It's seven in the morning
on Douglas Street.
I am blundering about the flat,
trying not to wake you,
looking for my keys,
already late for work.
I know I will eventually
have to ask you
and you will tell me
exactly where they are
but for now
I am fumbling through every
pouch and pocket
like a first-time burglar.
Defeated, I stand by the bedside,
steeling myself, preparing to wake you
and suddenly I'm on my knees,
pestering your sweet, sleeping face
with urgent kisses.

Three Rooms

after Cavafy

i

The room was tiny and airless,
perched above a dingy *taverna*.
Through its grimy window
you could make out the alley below
and hear the voices of the beggars,
as they traded minor epics of misery
to gusts of laughter.

But there on that unkempt bed
with the broken lamp-stand
and the flickering bulb,
we made love with such tenderness,
that even now, as I write,
so many years later,
I'm suffused with longing
all over again.

ii

That room, how well I recall it:
the couch near the door,
a frayed but genuine Persian carpet
spread in front of it,
the shelf to the left
with the two yellow vases
(never once with flowers
in all the time we stayed there),
the writing table next to the window beside the bed,
where we made love so long,
so well and so many times.

At four one afternoon we parted,
for a month, we proposed,
as a trial, we agreed,
and then...

iii

Walking yesterday in the old neighbourhood,
I passed the house
and that room of almost deranged passion.
How long is it since we spent every afternoon
of that prolonged summer in each others' arms?
And when I walked by again,
everything was suddenly illumined
in the glow of nostalgia.
Nothing, not even the grotty bus shelter,
could be anything other than beautiful
in that forgiving spotlight.

I must have stood there for half an hour,
radiating with remembered pleasure.

My Flirtation with International Socialism

On Douglas Street
an aromatic *Boeuf Bourguignon*
is simmering over a low flame
as we walk to the Off-Licence
to choose a sacrificial red.
Near Parliament Bridge,
in a sudden fit of passion,
or simply overcome with hunger,
you kiss the back of my right hand
three times in rapid succession,
taking me totally and delightedly unawares.
That moment of mutual,
wide-eyed affection remains undiminished
through all the elaborate spins
we have subsequently applied
to our brief affair.

Do Not Resuscitate

It was either builder's crack or serious cleavage
but something distracted me long enough for you
to slip by undetected with your freshly unwrapped
husband and your recently straightened, decidedly
bouffant hair. It was either a recurring ear infection
or age-related entropy but if you did chance a guarded
greeting I certainly didn't catch it, of course you may not
have opened your mouth, in fact you probably played dumb
for the simple reason of not wanting to raise uncomfortable
ghosts in broad daylight, then again if you did and you think
I was snubbing you, I wasn't, as you can see I didn't even
know you were there but if I had known I would have I
mean I wouldn't have I mean…

Actually I haven't a clue what you look like now,
it's been almost ten years since I saw you in the flesh
and I have been relying on second- and even third-hand
sightings, the latest of which confirms a certain filling-out,
though insisting on your continuing and indeed, deepening beauty,
but it seems the curls are gone, shorn and stashed away
with the fossilized remnants of International Socialism.
So if I am obsessing and I probably am, then I am obsessing
on someone who no longer exists phenomenally, aesthetically,
metaphysically, politically or romantically.

At some level, say ground-level, you begin to think:
I'm dealing with this, if not entirely successfully then
at least with enough emotional stability to keep everything
limping merrily along. Then, after falling asleep to the mad
lullaby of a frantically ticking clock, you are pulled down
into one of those rare, brilliantly-lit, head-clearing dreams
and you are given an inkling of how deep this lies,
how turbulent its waters, how fast they run.

Mayakovsky's 'Testament'

after Stephanie Schwerter

Our love boat
has run aground
on a sandbar
of the quotidian.
You and I are even.
There is nothing
to be gained
in compiling a list
of our manifest loss.
We loved well,
we parted well,
enough.

Particle Entanglement for Beginners

"What are you thinking about?" she whispered,
as we lay in the blissful aftermath.
"About you," I replied.
"Actually, to be specific, I'm thinking
about the astonishing interconnectedness of things,
and I mean everything, both before and after
the Big Bang or should I say the Great Expansion,
or perhaps even the Sudden Collapse
of the Steady State Universe,
and since you are an integral part of this process
at any given moment since Time kicked-in,
if only at a fundamental particle level,
then obviously I'm thinking about you,
in fact I'm always thinking about you,
indeed I cannot *not* think about you."
"Just checking," she murmured.

Rummaging through some old papers,
I turn up a mislaid photograph
taken some twenty years before.
You-know-who, young and undeniably gorgeous,
sitting against the crumbling tower wall
of some sun-struck Welsh redoubt.
She's giving the camera her "how the fuck does
this fool expect me to smile when he has me
looking directly into the sun. What the fuck have
I been doing for the past four years going out
with this gold-plated cretin? Have I been in a daze
or what? And the sex? Give me a fucking break,
after the weekly roll-on, roll-off, roll-over, I might
as well be sleeping with my sister. I was far better

off with my fingers. It's high time I gave this self-absorbed
wanker the old heave-ho. Four years, four fucking years,
I can't believe it! And no breaking it gently either,
straight-up-no-kiss, sling your hook slim, hit the road jack,
fuck you, you fucking fuck" look.

After the small-talk and the goodnight palaver,
I turned to leave and had taken three steps
towards the garden gate when you called me back,
saying it was bad luck to part without a kiss.
Then hitting me full on the mouth
with a bruising, closed-lipped osculation,
you knocked me backwards
into the white thorn's brutal embrace,
into the ineluctable clasp
of its bristling acupunctural array.

Wine, Love & Death

after Abu al-Hasan — for Peter Wise

That night,
however much we drank,
the wine jug refused to empty.
I staggered home at dawn
and surprised her,
tossing and turning
in a fitful sleep.
She let out a languorous sigh
as I swung her anklets
up over her shoulders
to jingle against her earrings.

In the midst of the struggle,
surrounded by infidels,
I had a flash-back of Suleima
and of that melancholy day
on which we parted.
I could have sworn
I saw her sinuous shape
in the thicket of lances
thrusting at me
and rode to embrace it.

A Thought from Propertius

after Yeats — for Kate McCormick

She might,
given those smooth flowing lines
from noble head to shapely feet,
have walked to the altar
through the sacred images
at Pallas Athena's side,
or, trussed and abandoned
on a forest path,
been fit sport for centaurs
inflamed with unmixed wines.

Bedside Manner

after Carson's 'Táin'

The first doctor approached
and examined Cethern.
"You won't last long," he told him.
"Then neither will you," said Cethern
and gave him such a punch
that his brains burst out through his ears.
Cethern dealt in similar fashion
with fifty doctors, one after the other.
The last received a glancing blow
and survived but was unable
to practice medicine again,
such was the damage to his brain,
and had to take up literature instead.

Haiku for Bonnie

after Lorca

The lizard asleep
one droplet of crocodile
on a yellow leaf.

Haiku for Deirdre

A blackbird singing
perched on the satellite dish
sweet interference.

Through the dripping leaves
the distant starry glitter
of the Pleiades.

In the moonlit pot
a lemon geranium
shakes with awareness.

The Seasons

for John Spillane

After wind and rain
we search beneath cherry trees
for apple blossom.

Searing afternoons
dust-devils on the pool deck
chasing their own tails.

An old retriever
padding through the fallen leaves
the hard road beckons.

First chill of winter
the late bee returns laden
to an empty hive.

Solstice

Peeking through the dusty fanlight
to strike the newel post
plumb on its polished centre-knot,
the haggard mid-winter sun.

The Childhood of Columbus

after Coleridge

Happily adrift
in his own painted boat
on his own painted ocean.

Still Out There

for Jean Marie Faley

Who knows
why Britt Sullivan,
a hard-drinking, former WAVE
from Nebraska,
decided to swim the Atlantic in 1964?
Somewhere off Fire Island,
twenty miles from her starting point,
she lost touch with her escort boat
and was never seen again.

Lost at Sea

after Simonides

From Sparta we sailed
with the first fruits of the season,
a gift for Apollo.
He accepted it
(and us)
as one great watery offering.

For the Poets

after Octavio Paz

Three minutes past three,
I scratch down a few lines,
the pen dragging its viscera
across the indifferent page,
a dismal trail of letters
glistening by lamplight.

On the Eve of his Eightieth Birthday

after Euripides — for John Montague

Hey! Who's next on watch?
We've done our stint.
The first planets to rise
are already setting,
the Pleiades are skimming
the glowing margin of heaven,
and the eagle is busily ranging
the mid-vault of the skies.
No nodding off,
up from your couches
and watch on!
The moon is still shining,
through the dawn is near.
Even now the morning-star approaches,
diffident but inexorable.

Tholla Bhriste

after James Humbert Craig — for Seamus Heaney

It wouldn't take much,
a slight transformation
into a loose conglomerate of oil colours,
to enter this.
The heather, still springy
despite a recent squall of rain
from those tatterdemalion clouds,
the turf cutters too absorbed in conversation
to notice you stride past,
skirting the edge of that improbably indigo lake,
climbing effortlessly over the foothills
and on into the purple distances
of the beckoning mountains.

The Age of Celebrity

Your tattered ghost flies past,
blown through the oak forest
like a page from a thousand-year-old tabloid.